O Holy Night
The First Christmas

Written by Makoto Yamamoto
Illustrated by Wakako Moritsu

Pauline
BOOKS & MEDIA
Boston

A long time ago, there was a young woman named Mary.
She lived in a small village called Nazareth.

One day, the Archangel Gabriel came to visit Mary.

Gabriel brought a message from God.

Gabriel said, "Hail Mary! God is always with you.

You are filled with grace."

Mary was very surprised.

But Gabriel said, "Do not be afraid.

You are going to have a baby boy.

You will name him **Jesus.**

He will be the Son of God, and he will make everyone happy."

Mary said, "I will do everything God wants."

Mary was going to marry Joseph.
Now Mary and Joseph were very busy.
They got everything ready
for the coming of Jesus.

Around that time, the king gave an order.
This is what he said: "Everyone has to go to
the town their family came from. I want to
count all the people in my kingdom."
Mary and Joseph had to go to Bethlehem.
Bethlehem was far away from Nazareth.

When Mary and Joseph got to Bethlehem,
it was full of people!
Mary and Joseph could not get a room in the hotel
that night.
And it was almost time for Jesus to be born!

Finally, Mary and Joseph found a place where animals lived.

They went inside.

Then Jesus, God's Son, was born!

Mary wrapped Baby Jesus up.

She put him in a manger.

A manger is something that holds food for animals.

Some shepherds were watching their sheep that night.

God sent an angel to see them.

The shepherds were so surprised!

The angel said, "Do not be afraid. The Savior is born!

He is the one who is going to make everyone happy. Go to

Bethlehem. You will find a baby sleeping in a manger.

He is the Savior."

Suddenly, many other angels filled the sky.

They were all praising God.

The shepherds hurried over to Bethlehem.
They found Baby Jesus sleeping in the manger,
just as the angel had told them.
Mary and Joseph were there too.
The shepherds were so happy!
They told everyone they met about Jesus, the Savior.
And, praising God, they went back to their sheep.

Other people found out the good news about the Savior too.

Far, far away, there were three Wise Men. They studied the stars.

They noticed one star that was very, very bright.

"If we follow this star, we will surely meet the Savior," they said.

The Wise Men got on their camels and followed the shiny star.

The star stopped over the place where Baby Jesus was.

The Wise Men met Jesus, Mary, and Joseph.

They were so happy! They knew that Jesus is our Savior.

They gave Jesus special gifts.

This is the story of that holy night when Jesus was born.

Christmas is a day to wish Jesus a happy birthday.

Jesus was born on the first Christmas night.

Now, Jesus lives in our hearts.

Thank you, Jesus, for loving me!

Thank you, Jesus, for living in my heart!

A Note to Parents and Teachers

While we celebrate December 25 as Christmas Day, we can say that every day is Christmas. This is true because Jesus, our Savior, has been born in each of our hearts. He lives within us to give us life. The day when we realize this will be the day we begin to live Christmas all year long.

May this book, which is about the first Christmas 2,000 years ago, inspire you and your children to reflect on the Savior's continuing birth in our lives.

Wishing you a Merry Christmas,

M. Yamamoto

Library of Congress Cataloging-in-Publication Data

Yamamoto, Makoto, priest.
  [Kurisumasu ga kitayo. English]
  O holy night : the first Christmas / written by Makoto Yamamoto;
illustrated by Wakako Moritsu.—1st English ed.
      p. cm.
  ISBN 0-8198-5440-9 (hardcover)
  1. Jesus Christ—Nativity—Juvenile literature. I. Moritsu, Wakako. II. Title.
  BT315.3.Y3613 2005
  232.92—dc22   2004025439

English adaptation by Patricia Edward Jablonski, FSP

Originally published in Japanese under the title *Christmas Has Come* by the Daughters of St. Paul, 12-42 Akasaka 8 Chome, Minatoku, Tokyo 107-0052

First English Edition, 2005

Copyright © 2002, Makoto Yamamoto and Wakako Moritsu / Joshi Pauro Kai (Daughters of St. Paul) Tokyo

Published by Pauline Books & Media, 50 Saint Pauls Avenue, Boston, MA 02130-3491.

Printed in Korea.

www.pauline.org

Pauline Books & Media is the publishing house of the Daughters of St. Paul, an international congregation of women religious serving the Church with the communications media.

1 2 3 4 5 6 7 8 9   11 10 09 08 07 06 05

Pauline
BOOKS & MEDIA

The Daughters of St. Paul operate book and media centers at the following addresses. Visit, call or write the one nearest you today, or find us on the World Wide Web, www.pauline.org

CALIFORNIA	3908 Sepulveda Blvd, Culver City, CA 90230	310-397-8676
	5945 Balboa Avenue, San Diego, CA 92111	858-565-9181
	46 Geary Street, San Francisco, CA 94108	415-781-5180
FLORIDA	145 S.W. 107th Avenue, Miami, FL 33174	305-559-6715
HAWAII	1143 Bishop Street, Honolulu, HI 96813	808-521-2731
	Neighbor Islands call:	866-521-2731
ILLINOIS	172 North Michigan Avenue, Chicago, IL 60601	312-346-4228
LOUISIANA	4403 Veterans Memorial Blvd, Metairie, LA 70006	504-887-7631
MASSACHUSETTS	885 Providence Hwy, Dedham, MA 02026	781-326-5385
MISSOURI	9804 Watson Road, St. Louis, MO 63126	314-965-3512
NEW JERSEY	561 U.S. Route 1, Wick Plaza, Edison, NJ 08817	732-572-1200
NEW YORK	150 East 52nd Street, New York, NY 10022	212-754-1110
	78 Fort Place, Staten Island, NY 10301	718-447-5071
PENNSYLVANIA	9171-A Roosevelt Blvd, Philadelphia, PA 19114	215-676-9494
SOUTH CAROLINA	243 King Street, Charleston, SC 29401	843-577-0175
TENNESSEE	4811 Poplar Avenue, Memphis, TN 38117	901-761-2987
TEXAS	114 Main Plaza, San Antonio, TX 78205	210-224-8101
VIRGINIA	1025 King Street, Alexandria, VA 22314	703-549-3806
CANADA	3022 Dufferin Street, Toronto, Ontario, Canada M6B 3T5	416-781-9131

¡También somos su fuente para libros, videos y música en español!